WEST · HIGHLANDS

COLIN BAXTER

30/5/86.
To remind you of your
beloved Scotland,

Clare. and Hazel.
xx.

RICHARD DREW PUBLISHING
GLASGOW

WIDE CONTRASTS IN THE SCENERY OF SCOTLAND ALWAYS IMPRESS THE VISITOR. WHERE ELSE CAN BE FOUND IN SO SMALL AN AREA MOUNTAINS, SAVAGE SEAS, ROUGH COASTS, WOODED VALLEYS, WILD MOORLAND, TUMBLING RIVERS AND FERTILE PLAINS? CHANGING PLAY OF LIGHT BROUGHT BY THE FICKLE CLIMATE ADDS MYSTERY TO THE SCOTTISH EXPERIENCE.

NO-ONE IN RECENT YEARS HAS CAPTURED THIS EVER-CHANGING VARIETY AS SENSITIVELY AS THE PHOTOGRAPHER, COLIN BAXTER, WHO HAS IN THIS SERIES SELECTED CERTAIN AREAS AND THEMES TO CONVEY THE RICH DIVERSITY OF SCOTLAND'S CITIES AND COUNTRYSIDE.

THE WEST HIGHLANDS, NORTH AND WEST OF THE RIVER CLYDE, ARE BORDERED BY A LONG, RAGGED COASTLINE. MOUNTAIN AND WILD MOOR MAY SEEM TO PREDOMINATE BUT GREEN VALLEYS AND WOODED HILLS INTERCHANGE RAPIDLY WITH THE WILDERNESS. THIS IS THE HOMELAND OF THE GAELIC CULTURE OF SCOTLAND AND MANY REMINDERS OF ITS TURBULENT HISTORY ARE TO BE FOUND IN THE GLENS AND SEA LOCHS.

KINGAIRLOCH,
LOCH LINNHE

STAC POLLY,
WESTER ROSS

TORRIDON,
WESTER ROSS

CUL MOR,
WESTER ROSS

LOCH MAREE,
WESTER ROSS

OVERLEAF:
LOCH LUBHAIR,
GLEN DOCHART

GLEANN GEAL,
MORVERN

BEINN AN DOTHAITH,
MOOR OF RANNOCH

BEINN SUIDHE,
LORN

GLEN CROE,
ARGYLL

LOCH GARRY,
LOCHABER

SHED,
SUTHERLAND

RKTON,
OCH CARRON

POST BOX,
GLEN ERROCHTY,
ATHOLL

WOODLAND

FROM STOB AN EAS,
LOOKING ACROSS
LOCH FYNE

FIRTH OF LORN

LOCH LONG,
ARGYLL

BEINN MHEADHOIN,
KINGAIRLOCH,
LOCH LINNHE

BEN NEVIS

QUINAG.
SUTHERLAND

LOCH NESS

OVERLEAF:
SUILVEN AT DUSK,
SUTHERLAND

BEINN A' BHEITHIR.
LORN

WEST HIGHLAND WAY,
NEAR
BRIDGE OF ORCHY

TORRIDON HILLS,
WESTER ROSS

LOCH MAREE,
WESTER ROSS

LOCH ETIVE,
LORN

FISHERMEN ON
LOCH AWE

LOCH AWE,
ARGYLL

LOCH VOIL,
STRATHYRE

BEN CRUACHAN,
ARGYLL

First Published 1986 by
RICHARD DREW PUBLISHING
6 CLAIRMONT GARDENS, GLASGOW, G3 7LW, SCOTLAND

Printed and bound in Great Britain by
Blantyre Printing and Binding Co. Ltd.

British Library Cataloguing in Publication Data

"West Highlands — (Experience Scotland)
1. Highlands (Scotland) — Description
and travel — Guide-books
I. Title   II. Series
914.11'804858   DA880.H7

ISBN 0-86267-155-8